2

Grace : The Fall From : Genesis Three.

By

John C Burt.

8

Photographs courtesy of :
 brigita - b
tim - marshall
 unsplash.com
 Free downloads from the
website .

9

1.

FOREWORD :

This book is called;
' Grace : The Fall From :
Genesis Three .'   My
thinking in writing a book on
the fall, is that , I have
already done a book on
' The Story of Creation ' and

14

I will be doing a book on ;
' Grace Restored : Romans 7
: 14 - 21 '. It would seem to
me that the two other books
flow out of the Story of
Creation and necessary to
visit if one wants to be true to
the very text of the Word of
God.

What I propose to do is to
consider the verses in
Genesis Three which outline
the story of the Fall of
Mankind in all it's graphic
detail . I sometimes wonder

if I had been in the position of Adam and Eve whether or not I would have done anything in a different fashion? On my best days I think I would still have made the same bad choices they both did before the gaze of the LORD GOD ALMIGHTY. You may well think if you were in their position you would not have made the very real choices they did but that is very much a debatable point. It is easy to be very wise with hindsight but it is when one is in the very situation and when one has to make the right choice that one really finds out what one is made of? So, therefore I would simply believe that any of us faced with the choices that both Adam and Eve had; would make the wrong choice as they did.

The interesting thing about the Fall and Genesis Three, is that, so much has been already been written on the subject. Also, the Fall itself has many cultural forms and even productions using it's concepts and by - play as a back drop to what they are trying to say. The Fall evokes many different feelings in different people, some would say it is just a made - up story and has no real value in explaining anything about mankind and the LORD GOD ALMIGHTY and their relationship and even it's

18

breakdown?

I would rather believe that the Fall and Genesis Three has much to say to us; if we would only see and hear it with unveiled eyes and hearts before the very gaze of the LORD GOD ALMIGHTY. This is the main premise of this very book regards the Fall and the whole of Genesis Three and their intrinsic value and worth, in an ongoing way and ways.

2a.

SCRIPTURAL
CITATIONS :

GENESIS 3.

(CEB)

(1) " The snake was the most intelligent of all the wild animals that the LORD God had made. He said to the woman, " Did God really say that you shouldn't eat from any tree in the garden?"

(2) The woman said to the snake, " We may

eat the fruit of the garden's trees

(3) but not the fruit of the tree in the middle of the garden. God said," Don't eat from it, and don't touch it, or you will die."

(4) The snake said to the woman, " You won't die!

(5) God knows that on the day you eat from it , you

will see clearly and you will be like God, knowing good and evil."

(6) The woman saw that the tree was beautiful with delicious food and that the tree would provide wisdom, so she took some of its fruit and ate it, and also gave some to he husband, who was with her, and he ate it.

(7) Then they both saw clearly and knew that they were naked. So they sewed fig leaves together and made garments for themselves.

(8) During that day's cool evening breeze, they heard the sound of the LORD God walking in the garden; and the man and his wife hid themselves from the LORD God in the middle of the garden's trees.

(9) The LORD God called to the man and said to him, " Where are you?"

(10) The man replied, " I heard your sound in the garden; I was afraid because I was naked, and I hid myself."

(11) He said,

" Who told you that you were naked? Did you eat from the tree, which I commanded you not to eat?"

(12) The man said, " The woman you gave me, she gave me some the tree, and I ate ."

(13) The LORD God said to the woman, " What have you done?!"

And the woman

said, " The snake tricked me,
and I ate."

(14) The LORD
God said to the snake,
" Because you
did this, you are the one
cursed out of all the farm
animals, out of all the wild
animals.

On your belly you
will crawl, and dust you will
eat every day of your life.

35

(15) I will put contempt between you and the woman, between your offspring and hers. They will strike your head, but you will strike at their heels."

(16) To the woman he said, " I will make your pregnancy very painful; in pain you will bear children. You will desire your husband, but he will rule over you."

(17) To the man he said, " Because you listened yo your wife's voice and you ate from the tree that I commanded,' You will not eat from it,'

cursed is the ground because of you;

in pain you will eat from it every day of your life.

(18) Weeds and thistles will grow for you,

even as you eat the field's
plants;

(19) by the
sweat of your face you will eat
bread - until you return to the
fertile land, since from it you
were taken; you are soil, to the
soils you will return."

(20) The man
named his wife Eve because
she is the mother of everyone
who lives.

38

(21) The LORD
God made the man and his
wife leather clothes and
dressed them.

(22) The LORD
God said, " The human being
has now become like one of
us, knowing good and evil.
Now so he doesn't stretch out
his hand and take also from
the tree of life and eat and live
forever,"

(23) the LORD God sent him out of the garden of Eden to farm the fertile land from which he was taken.

(24) He drove out the human. To the east of the garden of Eden, he stationed winged creatures wielding flaming swords to guard the way to the tree of life ."

2b.

Genesis Three:

(N I V)

(1) " Now the serpent was more crafty than any of the wild animals the LORD GOD had made. He said to the woman , " Did God

really say, ' You must not eat
from any tree in the garden.' ?"

(2) The woman
said to the serpent, " We may
eat fruit from the trees in the
garden,

(3) but God did
say , ' You must not eat fruit
from the tree that is in the
middle of the garden, and you
must not touch it, or you will
die.' "

(4) " You will not surely die," the serpent said to the woman.

(5) " For God knows that when you eat of it your eyes will be opened, and you will be like God, knowing good and evil."

(6) When the woman saw that the fruit of the tree was good for food and pleasing to the eye, and also desirable for gaining wisdom, she took some and ate it. She also gave some to her husband, who was with her, and he ate it."

(7) Then the eyes of both were opened, and they realized they were naked; so they sewed fig leaves together and made coverings for themselves.

(8) Then the man and his wife heard the sound of the LORD God as he was walking in the garden in the cool of the day, and they hid from the LORD God among the trees of the garden.

(9) But the LORD GOD called to the man, " Where are you? "

(10) He answered,

" I heard you in the garden, and I was afraid because I was naked; so I hid."

(11) And he said, " Who told you that you were naked? Have you eaten from the tree that I commanded you not to eat from? "

(12) The man said , " The woman you put me here with me - she gave me some fruit from the tree, and I ate it."

(13) Then the LORD God said to the woman, " What is this you have done?" The woman said, " The serpent deceived me , and I ate."

(14) So the LORD God said to the serpent, " Because you have done this,

" Cursed are you above all the livestock and all the wild animals!

You will crawl on your belly and you will eat dust all the days of your life.

(15) And I will put enmity between you and the woman, and between her offspring and hers; he will crush your head, and you will strike his heel."

(16) To the woman he said,

" I will greatly increase your pains in childbearing; with pain you will give birth to children.

Your desire will be for your husband, and he will rule over you."

(17) To Adam he said, " Because you listened to your wife and ate from the tree

about which I commanded
you, ' You must not eat of it ',
  " Cursed is the ground
because of you; through
painful toil you will eat of it all
the days of your life.

(18) It will
produce thorns and thistles for
you, and you will eat the
plants of the field.

(19) By the
sweat of your brow you will

eat your food until you return
to the ground,
        since from it you
were taken; for dust you are
 and to the dust you will
return."

(20) Adam named
his wife Eve, because she
would become the mother of
all the living.

(21) The LORD
God made garments of skin

60

for Adam and his wife and clothed them.

(22) And the LORD God said, " The man has now become like one of us, knowing good and evil. He must not be allowed to reach out his hand and take also from the tree of life and eat, and live forever."

(23) So the LORD God banished him from the

Garden of Eden to work the ground from which he had been taken.

(24) After he drove the man out, he placed on the east side of the Garden of Eden cherubim and a flaming sword flashing back and forth to guard the way to the tree of life. "

63

2c.

Genesis Three :

(E S V)

(1) " Now the
serpent was more crafty than
any other beast of the field
that the LORD God had
made. He said to the woman,

" Did God actually say, ' You shall not eat of any tree in the garden'? "

(2) And the woman said to the serpent, " We may eat of the fruit of the trees in the garden,

(3) but God said, ' You shall not eat of the fruit of the tree that is in the midst of the garden, neither shall you

73

touch it, lest you die."

(4) But the
serpent said to the woman,
" You will not surely die.

(5) For God
knows that when you eat of it
your eyes will be opened ,
and you will be like God,
knowing good and evil."

(6) So when the
woman saw that the tree was

good for food, and that it was a delight to the eyes, and that the tree was to be desired to make one wise, she took of its fruit and ate, and she also gave some to her husband who was with her, and he ate.

(7) Then the eyes of both were opened, and they knew that they were naked. And they sewed fig leaves together and made themselves loincloths.

(8) And they heard the sound of the LORD God walking in the garden in the cool of the day, and the man and his wife hid themselves from the presence of the LORD God among the trees of the garden.

(9) But the LORD God called to the man and said to him, " Where are you? "

(10) And he said,
" I heard the sound of you in the garden, and I was afraid, because I was naked, and I hid myself."

(11) He said, " Who told you that you were naked? Have you eaten of the tree of which I commanded you not to eat? "

(12) The man said,

" The woman whom you gave to be with me, she gave me fruit of the tree, and I ate ."

(13) Then the LORD God said to the woman, " What is this that you have done?" The woman said , " The serpent deceived me, and I ate."

(14) The LORD God said to the serpent, " Because you have done this, cursed are you above

all livestock
    and above all beasts of
the field;
    on your belly you shall
go,
    and the dust you shall
eat all the days of your life.

    (15) I will put
enmity between you and the
woman, and between your
offspring and her offspring; he
shall bruise your head, and
you shall bruise his heel."

(16) To the woman he said,

" I will surely multiply your pain in childbearing; in pain you shall bring forth children.

Your desire shall be contrary to your husband, but he shall rule over you."

(17) And to Adam he said ,

" Because you have listened to the voice of your wife and have eaten of the tree of which I commanded you, ' You shall not eat of it,' cursed is the ground because of you; in pain you shall eat of it all the days of your life;

(18) thorns and thistles it shall bring forth for you; and you shall eat the plants of the field.

(19) By the sweat of your face you shall eat bread, till you return to the ground, for out of it you were taken; for you are dust, and to dust you shall return."

(20) The man called his wife's name Eve, because she was the mother of all living.

(21) And the LORD God made for Adam and for his wife garments of skins and clothed them.

(22) Then the LORD God said, " Behold, the man has become like one of us in knowing good and evil. Now, lest he reach out his hand and take also of the tree of life and eat, and live forever - "

(23) therefore the LORD God sent him out from the garden of Eden to work the ground from which he was taken.

(24) He drove out the man, and at the east of the garden of Eden he placed the cherubim and a flaming sword that turned every way to guard the way to the tree of life."

85

2d.

Genesis Three :

(G N T)

(1) " Now the snake was the most cunning animal that the LORD God had made. The snake asked the woman, " Did God really tell you not to eat fruit from any tree in the garden? "

(2) " We may eat the fruit of any tree in the garden," the woman answered,

(3) " except the tree in the middle of it. God told us not to eat the fruit of that tree or even touch it; if we do, we will die."

(4) The snake

replied, " That's not true; you will not die.

(5) God said that because he knows that when yo eat it, you will be like God and know what is good and what is bad."

(6) The woman saw how beautiful the tree was and how good its fruit would be to eat, and she thought how wonderful it would be to become wise. So she took some of the fruit and ate it. Then she gave some to her husband, and he also ate it.

(7) As soon as they had eaten it; they were given understanding and realized that they were naked; so they sewed fig leaves together and covered themselves.

(8) That evening they heard the LORD God walking in the garden, and they hid from him among the trees.

(9) But the LORD God called out to the man, " Where are you? "

(10) He answered, " I heard you in the garden; I was afraid and hid from you, because I was naked."

(11) " Who told you that you were naked?" God asked. " Did you eat the fruit that I told you not to eat?"

(12) The man answered, " The woman you put me here with me gave me the fruit, and I ate it."

(13) The LORD God asked the woman, " Why did you do this ? " She replied, " The snake tricked me into eating it."

(14) Then the LORD God said to the snake, " You will be punished for this; you alone of all the animals must bear this curse: From now on you will crawl on your belly, and you will have to eat dust as long as you live.

(15) I will make you and the woman hate each other; her offspring and yours will always be enemies. Her offspring will crush your head, and you will bite her offspring's heel."

(16) And he said to the woman, " I will increase your trouble in pregnancy and your pain in giving birth. In spite of this, you will still have desire for your husband, yet you will be subject to him."

(17) And he said to the man,

" You listened to your wife and ate the fruit which I told you not to eat. Because of what you have done, the ground will be under a curse. You will have to work hard all your life to make it produce enough food for you.

(18) It will produce weeds and thorns,

102

and you will have to eat wild plants.

(19) You will have to work hard and sweat to make the soil produce anything, until you go back to the soil from which you were formed. You were made from soil, and you will become soil again."

(20) Adam named his wife Eve, because she was

the mother of all human beings.

(21) And the LORD God made clothes out of animal skins for Adam and his wife, and he clothed them.

(22) Then the LORD God said, " Now these human beings have become like one of us and have knowledge of what is good and what is bad. They must not be allowed to take fruit from the tree that gives life, eat it, and live forever."

(23) So the LORD God sent them out of the Garden of Eden and made them cultivate the soil from which they had been formed.

(24) Then at the east side of the garden he put living creatures and a flaming sword which turned in all directions. This was to keep anyone from coming near the tree that gives life."

107

3.

Genesis 3 : 1 - 6.

(E S V)

(1) " Now the serpent was more crafty than any other beast of the field that the LORD God had made. He said to the woman, " Did God actually say, ' You shall not eat of any tree in the garden'? "

(2) And the woman said to the serpent, " We may eat of the fruit of the trees in the garden,

(3) but God said, " You shall not eat of the fruit of the tree that is in the midst of the garden, neither shall you touch it, lest you die. "

(4) But the serpent said to the woman, " You will not surely die.

(5) For God knows that when you eat of it your eyes will be opened, and you will be like God, knowing good and evil. "

(6) So when the woman saw that the tree was good for food, and that it was a delight to the eyes, and that the tree was to be desired to make one wise, she took of its fruit and ate, and she also gave some to her husband who was with her, and he ate. "

Genesis 3 : 1 - 6.

(G N T)

(1) " Now the snake was the most cunning animal that the LORD God had made. The snake asked the woman,

" Did God really tell you not to eat fruit from any tree in the garden? "

(2) " We may eat the fruit of any tree in the garden, " the woman answered,

(3) " except the tree in the middle of it. God told us not to eat the fruit of that tree or even touch it; if we do, we will die. "

(4) The snake replied , " That's not true; you will not die.

(5) God said that because he knows that when you eat it, you will be like God and know what is good and what is bad. "

(6) The woman saw how beautiful the tree was and how good its fruit would be to eat, and she thought how wonderful it would be to become wise. So she took some of the fruit and ate it. Then she gave some to her husband, and he also ate it. "

In verse one, we have the intrusion of evil in the form of a talking snake into the very paradise of the Garden of Eden. As you would know, snakes do not talk; and so we have Satan , the Devil talking through the snake to the woman.

The LORD God had placed both the woman and the man in the Garden of Eden. It's is in so many ways an abrupt intrusion of evil an wrong doing into the paradise of the Garden of Eden, as had been created for the man and woman created by the LORD GOD ALMIGHTY to live in. The narrative of Genesis Three does not tell us much about the mechanics of how and why evil made it's intrusion into the paradise of the Garden of Eden? It

123

rather just informs us that there is a snake that is talking to the woman , now in the paradise of the Garden of Eden.

There is an emphasis on the fact and the reality that the snake had in been created by the LORD GOD ALMIGHTY Himself. The snake was the high point of the creation of the things that creep along the ground, that had been created by the LORD GOD ALMIGHTY. The thing that is interesting, is that, it was the LORD GOD Himself who created the snake to be both cunning and crafty (as per the ESV translation.) Therefore , what happens after verse one is a misuse of its created purpose and design? It becomes a tool in the hands of Satan, and he uses it's cunning and craftiness for his own ends.

In verse one we see the beginnings of any and all disobedience in terms of the commands and words of the LORD GOD ALMIGHTY. That which seeks to question whether He in fact said what He did say in His commands and very word and words to people? The talking snake is attempting to drive a wedge between what the LORD GOD ALMIGHTY actually said and what he wanted the woman to believe He had said to herself and the man in the Garden of Eden. Through all of this we can see the cunning talking snake attempting to throw some doubt and confusion into the mind and heart of the woman created by the LORD GOD ALMIGHTY resident in the Garden of Eden.

Some times that's all it takes for us to turn away from and for us to disbelieve the very commands and words of the LORD GOD ALMIGHTY to us. Some small doubts and some small questioning of what the LORD GOD ALMIGHTY has really said.

All of this leads to the reply to the talking snake of the woman. She states what she believes the LORD GOD ALMIGHTY has in fact said to herself and the man regarding the fruit of the trees in the Garden of Eden. She details what she thinks He has said about what they can eat and what they cannot eat the fruit of. The talking snake has led the woman to highlight the reality that they were not allowed in reality to eat all of the fruits of every tree in the Garden of Eden. There is a tree right in the middle of the very Garden of Eden that they are forbidden by the LORD GOD ALMIGHTY from eating it's fruit. The reality, is that, if they eat of the fruit of this particular tree , they have been told by the LORD God that they will die.

In verse four; the talking snake seizes upon what the woman has just said about dying if they eat of the fruit of the tree in the middle of the Garden of Eden. (G N T)

(4) " The snake replied, " That's not true; you will not die. " The snake flat rejects what the LORD GOD ALMIGHTY has in fact said would happen to the man and woman if they ate of the fruit of the tree in the middle of the Garden of

Eden. His reply makes the woman doubt, question and plants the seeds of her own rejection of what the LORD GOD ALMIGHTY had said about the tree in the middle of the Garden of Eden. All of this is heightened in verse five when the talking snake states further reasons as to why the LORD GOD ALMIGHTY has said what He has said regards the tree in the middle of the Garden of Eden. (G N T

131

v 5) " God said that because he knows that when you eat it, you will be like God and know what is good and what is bad. " This is in fact a verse which is at the heart of the fall from grace in the Garden of Eden by the man and the woman.

The man and the woman desire to become like God; to be God - like, it introduces the idea of them no longer being happy just being creatures created by the LORD GOD

132

Almighty. They now want to be like the Creator God and know the difference between good and evil. The question that arises out of all of this; is did the man and the woman understand good and evil before this, it would seem that they did not understand before they ate of the tree in the middle of the garden of Eden.

This is really important to see; it is the crux of the fall from grace of the LORD GOD ALMIGHTY in the garden of

Eden. In reality it was in seeking to be like the LORD GOD ALMIGHTY; to be God - like themselves. So it's not only that they disobey the very commands and words of the LORD GOD ALMIGHTY but also that they desire to be God - like.

This is very interesting and for some of you may bring some revelation as to what really Genesis Three is all about ; at it's heart. The further interesting thing, is that , the man and the woman were made to be the pinnacle of the created order and here they are trying to usurp the LORD GOD ALMIGHTY and His position as the Creator God. In doing this and seeking to do this they fall very short of what they were in reality created to be and do? It's like being the very pinnacle of the created order was not enough for them and could never be enough for them?

Verse six shows the actions of the woman after her discussions with the snake who talks. She admires the fruit and then take some of it and eats it and then she also takes some of it and gives it to her husband to eat as well. In this verse we see the fulfillment of the both the desires of the snake who talks but also of those of both the man and the woman in eating the fruit

from the tree , they were
forbidden to eat from by
the LORD GOD. They go
against the very commands
and the very words of the
LORD GOD ALMIGHTY to
them both about the tree at
the middle of the Garden of
Eden and it's fruit. They
both end up doing what
they should not be doing;
they eat of the tree in the
middle of the Garden of
Eden.

4.

Genesis 3 : 7 - 12.

(CEB)

(7) " Then they both saw clearly and knew that they were naked. So they sewed fig leaves

together and made
garments for themselves.

(8) During the
day's cool evening breeze,
they heard the sound of
the LORD God walking in
the garden, and the man
and his wife hid
themselves from the
LORD God in the middle
of the garden's trees.

(9) The
LORD God called to the
man and said to him ,

" Where are you ? "

(10) The man replied, " I heard your sound in the garden; I was afraid because I was naked, and I hid myself."

(11) He said , " Who told you that you were naked? Did you eat from the tree, which I commanded you not to eat?"

(12) The man said , " The woman

you gave me, she gave me
some fruit from the tree,
and I ate it. "

Genesis 3 : 7 - 12.

(N I V)

(7) " Then the
eyes of both of them were
opened, and they realized
they were naked; so they
sewed fig leaves together
and made coverings for

themselves.

(8) Then the man and his wife heard the sound of the LORD God as he was walking in the garden in the cool of the day, and they hid from the LORD God among the trees of the garden.

(9) But the LORD God called to the man, " Where are you? "

(10) He

answered , " I heard you in the garden, and I was afraid because I was naked; so I hid. "

(11) And he said, " Who told you that you were naked? Have you eaten from the tree that I commanded you not to eat from? "

(12) The man said, " The woman you put here with me - she gave me some fruit from the tree , and I ate it. "

Verse seven is the
' ah ha ' moment in the
narrative of the Fall of
Mankind , that is Genesis
Three : 1 - 24. After the
man and woman eat from
the tree that they were not
allowed to by the LORD
GOD ALMIGHTY; they very
suddenly and abruptly
come to the realization
that they are both naked
before each other. From
the text of the verse , it
would seem before they
had eaten of the fruit of

this tree they had no awareness of them being naked before each other?

Here we see the intrusion of self-consciousness, shame and the desire of wanting to hide from the very nakedness of one's own body. All of these things had not been existent in the creation and the Garden of Eden before the man and the woman ate of the fruit of the tree in the middle of the Garden of Eden. It's the very moment when the innocence and even the seemingly perfection of the creation; as was created by the LORD GOD ALMIGHTY is seemingly lost and changed in a negative sense and way. The man and the woman had been very comfortable with each other, they had not been aware of their own bodies and even their own nakedness , now suddenly and abruptly all of that changes in the very blink of an eye.

In many ways verse

154

seven is the watershed moment of this section of verses; verse seven to twelve. From here on; things in this chapter will go downhill and a confrontation between the man and the woman and the LORD GOD ALMIGHTY is inevitable? After verse seven, it would seem as if the narrative itself pauses and takes a breath. It's as if it too is awaiting the confrontation between the LORD GOD ALMIGHTY

and the man and the
woman. The stress of the
narrative , is that, the
newly - found awareness
that the man and the
woman have of their own
nakedness is in and of
itself not a good thing that
has taken place in the
narrative thus far of the
episode in the Garden of
Eden.

If the man and the
woman were now naked
before each other's gaze;
then they were now naked

156

before the very gaze of the LORD GOD ALMIGHTY. So, we now have the introduction of shame and being self - conscious about the very nakedness of one's own body.

The narrative then drives along at breakneck speed and the LORD GOD ALMIGHTY is introduced into the very narrative of the chapter. He is found to be walking in the very Garden of Eden. All of which hints at the unbroken , undefined and constant access that the man and the woman had to and with the LORD GOD ALMIGHTY in the very Garden of Eden. All of which changes abruptly as the narrative develops further in Genesis Three : 1 - 24.

After the watershed moment in the narrative and the abrupt realization of their own nakedness by the man and the woman in verse seven. This relationship between the

LORD GOD ALMIGHTY
and the man and the
woman will never again
be the same , or so we
may think at this point in
the wider narrative of the
Word of God. There is no
real way back for the
man and the woman the
very real realization of
their own nakedness
before each other and the
LORD GOD ALMIGHTY is
clear cut evidence that
they have in fact
disobeyed the commands

of the LORD GOD and eaten from the tree in the middle of the Garden of Eden. They have not obeyed and done the right thing in terms of the words and the commands of the LORD GOD ALMIGHTY to them both.

The narrative then takes a twist we might not expected and foreseen? The first couple hide from the LORD GOD ALMIGHTY in their very nakedness. They do not want Him to see them in their very nakedness. Not only do they both not want to see each other's nakedness but they also do not want to be seen in their nakedness by their very Creator LORD GOD ALMIGHTY, at all costs. It would seem as one reads the narrative of this chapter, that the first couple had no reason to hide from the LORD GOD ALMIGHTY other than their own newly - found awareness of their own nakedness before Him.

There is a sense
in which they are both
vulnerable to each other
and to the LORD GOD
ALMIGHTY; in their very
nakedness before each
other and the LORD GOD.
So, we have the
introduction of the feeling
of being vulnerable to each
other in their own
nakedness and to the LORD
GOD ALMIGHTY as well.
The stress in the very
narrative of this chapter;

would seem to lend itself to the idea, notion and the very concept of the newly found and realized vulnerability not always having been present in the very creation and in the environment of the Garden of Eden itself.

Everything hinges upon the newly found awareness of the man and the woman and the LORD GOD ALMIGHTY rightly asks the man how he became aware of his nakedness? The very simple innocence

of the creation, the very
Garden of Eden and even
the created order has now
be shattered and destroyed
and changed forever. The
very things that the LORD
GOD ALMIGHTY had not
brought into the creation,
the created order and the
Garden of Eden itself have
now come into all three
things.

The LORD GOD
ALMIGHTY is now sure
that the man and the
woman have disobeyed His
commands and words to

them regarding the tree and it's fruit in the middle of the Garden of Eden? He expressly told them and commanded them both not to eat of the fruit of the tree in the middle of the Garden of Eden and now they have done what He had told them not to. Things will now never be the same again in the pristine, unadulterated creation , the Garden of Eden. The choice of the man and the woman to eat the forbidden fruit has now changed things forever? It changed things forever for both the man and the woman and even their relationship with the LORD GOD ALMIGHTY in the pristine, virgin and good Garden of Eden and for the whole of the creation and the created order as well.

Verse twelve contains the response of the man Adam to very probing questioning of himself by the LORD GOD ALMIGHTY. The LORD GOD just wants to know where the man is?

In this very verse and in his answer to the questioning of the LORD GOD ALMIGHTY, the man Adam appears to put the blame for what has happened in the Garden of Eden upon both the woman and even the LORD GOD ALMIGHTY Himself. He firstly blames the woman but he notes it is in fact the very woman that the LORD GOD ALMIGHTY has placed beside Him in the very Garden of Eden, that has

167

done these things.

Thus far, in the narrative of this chapter of the book of Genesis, there has been a hint that the man Adam was around as his wife talked to the talking snake and as she went to the tree in the middled of the Garden of Eden? He was around, or at least was aware of what was actually taking place in the very Garden of Eden. Therefore , he cannot claim to have no knowledge of what was taking place around himself, as he does seemingly in verse twelve. He would have had some awareness of the talking snake, what he was saying, the words and the actions of the woman in the Garden of Eden. Also, it has to be noted that when Adam is offered the fruit by the woman in the Garden of Eden he doe snot refuse it?

5.

Genesis 3 : 13 - 18.

(E S V)

(13) " Then the LORD God said to the woman. " What is this you have done? " The

woman said, " The serpent
deceived me and I ate. "

(14) The LORD
God said to the serpent,
" Because you
have done this, cursed are
you above livestock and
above all beasts of the
field; on your belly you
shall go, and dust you shall
eat all the days of your
life.

(15) I will put
enmity between you and
the woman, and between

your offspring and her offspring; he shall bruise your head, and you shall bruise his heel. "

(16) To the woman he said, " I will surely multiply your pain in childbearing; in pain you shall bring forth children. Your desire shall be contrary to your husband, and he shall rule over you. "

(17) And to Adam he said, " Because you have listened to the

180

voice of your wife and have
eaten of the tree of which I
commanded you,
' You shall not eat of it'
 cursed is the ground
because of you; in pain you
eat of it all the days of your
life;

        (18) thorns and
thistles it shall bring forth
for you; and you shall eat
the plants of the field. "

Genesis 3 : 13 - 18.
(GNT)

(13) " The LORD God asked the woman, " Why did you do this? " She replied, " The snake tricked me into eating it. "

(14) Then the LORD God said to the snake, " You will be punished for this : you alone of all the animals must bear this curse: From now on you will crawl on your belly and you will have to eat dust as long as you live.

(15) I will make you and the woman hate each other; her offspring and yours will always be enemies. Her offspring will crush your head, and you will bite her offspring's heel. "

(16) And he said to the woman, ' I will increase your trouble in pregnancy and your pain in giving birth. In spite of this, you will still have desire for your husband, yet you will be subject to him."

(17) And he said to the man,
" You listened to your wife and ate the fruit which I told you not to eat. Because of what you have done , the ground will be under a curse. You will have to work hard all your life to make it produce enough food for you.

(18) It will produce weeds and thorns and you will have to eat wild plants."

The questioning of the LORD God now turns to the woman. He wants to see what she has to say about what has happened with the eating of the forbidden fruit? In some ways, the question that the LORD God asks the woman points to the fact that He believes the man , Adam and what he has said happened with the eating of the fruit from the forbidden tree. " Why did you do this?" She replied, " The snake tricked me into eating it. " (GNT v 13) The woman disavows any personal involvement in the very act of eating the forbidden fruit and instead puts the blame for her actions on the talking snake? She says (GNT v 13 b) ' The snake tricked me into eating it.' Therefore, according to the woman's version of the events surrounding the eating of the forbidden fruit, she is not responsible because the ' snake 'tricked ' her into eating it.' To a degree, this is actually true, the talking snake or Satan or the Devil had in fact used smooth talking and persuasive words to make the woman doubt what the LORD GOD ALMIGHTY had in fact regarding the eating of the forbidden fruit.

In the end yet, the man and the woman are responsible in the very eyes of the LORD GOD for what they have done in eating the forbidden fruit. They were clearly forbidden from eating the fruit of this very tree in the middle of the Garden of Eden; it not good enough to blame the snake or to blame each other for their own actions and very real moral failure to do what the LORD GOD had commanded and instructed them to do.

In some ways, the woman is simply doing what her husband has already done in seeking to shift the blame for his own actions in eating the fruit of the forbidden tree. It is like both the man who has gone before her and herself do not want to even admit or even entertain the reality of their own failure and their own responsibility for it happening. In this the woman is not dealing with her unstated motivation, that we as the reader's of the text understand but that which she has not stated to the LORD GOD ALMIGHTY.

As you would remember the text says she wanted to be both wise and have wisdom and to be God-like in the end. These were her real motivations for her eating of the forbidden fruit. It's like she wants to avoid the truth of all of this and paint a very different picture of the reality of what actually took place in the eating of the forbidden fruit?

The majority of the verse in this section are caught up with the very words of the LORD GOD ALMIGHTY of judgment and his verdict upon those involved in the incident of the eating of the forbidden fruit. He judges the talking snake, the woman and then the man Adam. One wonders whether or not there is something in the very order of the verdicts and judgments? Does the LORD GOD ALMIGHTY; in fact hold the talking snake aka. Satan and the Devil more responsible than the woman or the man?

Any way, the LORD GOD ALMIGHTY pronounces judgment upon the talking snake first. It must be said from the outset that there is a bit of blur in the very text between the actual snake being judged and Satan or the Devil being judged by the LORD GOD ALMIGHTY? The verdict against the snake is that he will be cursed in ways that he other animals of creation will not be cursed. It will crawl upon it's very

belly in the dust of the
earth and wile in fact eat
the very dust of the earth
for the term of it's
natural life. Before this ,
in verse one, it seemed
like the snake who was
both cunning and crafty
had in fact been seen as a
high point of the creation
and the very animals that
had in fact been created
by the LORD GOD
ALMIGHTY.

In verse
fifteen ; there is also a

verdict and judgment
which has to do with the
relationship between the
very offspring of the
snake and those of the
woman. They will always
be an enmity between
their two offspring. This is
true of our days and our
generations , people
simply do not get along
too well with snakes and
vice versa.

There are many
who would seem the
verdict and judgment
against the snake as in

194

part referring to the works of the Lord Jesus Christ upon the very Cross of Calvary. They see it in terms of what He did to Satan and the Devil through the very Cross of Calvary and what He will ultimately do to him when He comes again. There is a swing between real snakes and the Devil and Satan but when it talks about crushing the head of the serpent it is obviously referring to the works of the Lord Jesus Christ.

The part about the serpent or snake biting the heel of the offspring of the woman may also have to do with the very death of the Lord Jesus Christ upon the Cross of Calvary. The reality, is that, the Lord Jesus Christ did in reality, suffer physical death from the Cross. It might well be this that is the bruising of the heel of the offspring of the woman.

In verse sixteen we have the verdict or the

pronouncement of judgment against the woman who ate of the forbidden fruit of the tree in the middle of the Garden of Eden. The main punishment for the woman , is that, now she will have lots of pain in childbirth and through her pregnancy. This is also true in our day and in our generations, women do have a lot of pain in childbirth and through out their pregnancies.

The second half of verse sixteen seems to point to the reality of there being now some friction in the very relationship between the woman and her husband. The woman will still have the sexual desire for her husband and to have children by him and yet there will also be problems in the relationship as well. There will be some consequences for the relationship between the man and the woman , the husband and his wife, their relationship will be affected adversely in some ways by the actions of the first couple Adam and his wife who later named Eve. These consequences from the first couple play out in the very relationships between husband's and their wife's today and are due to the very choices of the first couple on the planet Adam and Eve.

Verse seventeen and eighteen contain the

verdict and the judgment against Adam as per the ESV translation. Unlike the other verdicts and judgments this one has the very name of the first man, that is he is called by his name Adam. In many ways this calling him by his name seems to make it much more personal , a personal thing between the LORD GOD ALMIGHTY and the man called Adam.

In some ways it could even be argued that the LORD GOD ALMIGHTY holds the man , Adam to more account for what has happened in the eating of the forbidden fruit of the tree in the middle of the Garden of Eden. This is seen in the extreme punishment that the man , Adam receives for what he did in eating the fruit of the forbidden fruit. The very ground and the earth

of the planet is cursed
because of his own moral
failure.

Adam the man,
made the choice to eat for
himself and he also made
the choice to listen to his
wife , Eve rather than to
listen and obey the
commands and the words of
the LORD GOD ALMIGHTY.
The stress in the text would
seem to lie in the reality
that he should have listened
to the words and the very
commands of the LORD GOD
Almighty rightly. He failed

to do this and therefore
was judged by the LORD
GOD ALMIGHTY for his
own moral failure and his
failure to simply obey the
words and commands of
the LORD GOD ALMIGHTY.
The stress in the text
would seem to lie in the
very reality of the man,
Adam having made a real
choice and not one that was
in fact forced upon him by
the woman and the talking
snake; Adan himself made
the wrong choice and he
did not choose to obey the

very words and commands of the LORD GOD ALMIGHTY to himself and the woman.

In some ways, the verdict and judgment against Adam , the man , of cursing of the earth and the very ground of the planet would seen to be a bit harsh. It has had a lot of consequences for both the planet and mankind in general. There is a principle of the Word of God on show in this, and that is that, wrong doing and moral failure in terms of the things of the LORD GOD ALMIGHTY has consequences far beyond just the person involved in the act of failure. The effects and the very consequences of the failure can and will spill over and have some effects on the lives of other people not involved in the act of moral failure? It also has effects upon the creation and the created order of the planet earth as well.

The point , is that, in the end moral failure of any sort is not isolated in itself or cut off from the people and the creation that surrounds the person. There is within the text a linkage between one sphere or realm of the creation and humankind and moral failure of any sort. The point , is that, in the end the choices Adam , the man made had some very real consequences for himself, all of later humankind and the creation and the created order as well. Everything has been affected by the moral failure of both the man Adam and the woman later known as Eve. Therefore, the verdict s and the judgments given by the LORD GOD ALMIGHTY against the snake, the woman and the man Adam have had effects on so much in our world and the creation itself.

6.

Genesis 3 : 19 - 24.

(C E B)

(19) " by the sweat of your face you will eat bread - until you return to the fertile land, since from it you were taken, you are soil, to the soil you will return."

(20) "The man named his wife Eve". because she is the mother of everyone who lives.

(21) The LORD God made the man and his wife leather clothes and dressed them.

(22) The LORD God said, " The human being has now become like one of us, knowing good

and evil. Now so he
doesn't stretch out his
hand and take also from
the tree of life and eat and
live forever,"

(23) the
LORD God sent him out of
the garden of Eden to
farm the fertile land from
which he was taken.

(24) He drove
out the human. To the
east of the garden of
Eden, he stationed winged

creature wielding flaming swords to guard the way to the tree of life. "

Genesis 3 : 19 - 24.

(N I V)

(19) " By the sweat of your brow you will eat your food until you return to the ground, since from it you were taken;

for dust you are and to dust you will return. "

(20) Adam named his wife Eve, because she would become the mother of all the living.

(21) The LORD God made garments of skin for Adam and his wife and clothed them.

(22) And the LORD God said, " The man

has now become like one of us, knowing good and evil. He must not be allowed to reach out his hand and take also from the tree of life and eat, and live forever. "

(23) So the LORD God banished him to work the ground from which he had been taken.

(24) After he drove the man out , he placed on the east side of

the Garden of Eden
cherubim and a flaming
sword flashing back and
forth to guard the way to
the tree of life."

Verse nineteen
contains the last verdict
against the man Adam
from the LORD GOD
ALMIGHTY. Essentially the
man Adam will return to
the soil when he
eventually dies, ' dust to
dust '. In this there is no
hope of eternal life that is

on show; it is to the very dust that the man Adam will return, whence he came from, he will return to. It appears that death and dying has also come into the Garden of Eden and the life of the man , Adam. One can wonder if it was present in the Garden of Eden before the man and the woman morally failed to do the right thing in relation to the commands and the words of the LORD GOD ALMIGHTY regards the tree in the middle of the Garden of Eden and the eating of it fruit.

Verse twenty is also interesting, in that, it is the man Adam who actually names his wife, the woman Eve. Up until he does this the woman has largely been nameless and just a figure in the ongoing narrative of the chapter itself. Also, it is interesting that it is the man, Adam who actually names the woman rather than the LORD GOD ALMIGHTY Himself naming her. The man Adam had been named by the LORD GOD ALMIGHTY but in the case of the woman , she is given her name by the man, her husband. In some ways, this may signify that the man is responsible for the woman and is thus charged by the LORD GOD ALMIGHTY to have this responsibility before Him.

The reality, is that, all the living things, people come and begin from the

woman known as Eve. All
of which is very interesting
given the reality that she
will now have pain in both
pregnancy and childbirth.
Life and human beings
have there Genesis point
from this woman Eve.
Therefore; in some ways, it
would seem that the LORD
GOD ALMIGHTY while he
may well have judged the
woman , the snake and the
man Adam still has plans
and purposes for the
woman Eve. Eve the
woman of Genesis Three

has not been totally wiped out or even forgotten. The reality , is that, the plans of the LORD GOD ALMIGHTY for the whole of the human race are still in operation, the LORD has not gone to another plan or means or way of doing things. Eve, the woman of Genesis Three will still be the mother of all living things and human beings. The LORD GOD still has plans to fill the earth through this woman with human beings. one may well have thought that she would have been invalidated from doing this by her own moral failure to do what the LORD GOD ALMIGHTY had in fact commanded her to do .

Yet we see the grace and love and mercy of the LORD GOD ALMIGHTY towards both the woman and the future people of the world. The thing to keep in mind , is that , the LORD GOD ALMIGHTY does not have to show the woman, Eve, this mercy, love and grace, He could have found another way of doing what He planned to do with the whole of the human race.

This mercy, love and grace can be clearly seen in verse twenty - one where the LORD GOD ALMIGHTY clothes the man, Adam and his wife Eve. The LORD GOD ALMIGHTY makes provision for them both regards their own newly found and realized nakedness before Himself and each other. In this very provision of clothes for both Adam and Eve we see very well the very real provision of the LORD GOD ALMIGHTY for the first couple. Again, it is the sovereign choice of the LORD GOD ALMIGHTY that we see, He does not have to do what He does in clothing both Adam and Eve. He rather chooses to show then mercy, love and grace despite their own moral failure before Him. So, in some ways the LORD GOD ALMIGHTY can be seen to be overturning the moral failure of the man, Adam and the woman, Eve. He is mitigating the consequences of their own actions upon their own lives. So therefore ; in the end the moral failure 's of both the man, Adam and his wife Eve, do not have the final say over both their own futures and the plans of the LORD GOD ALMIGHTY for the future as well.

231

Verses 22, 23 and 24 reveal that the LORD GOD ALMIGHTY does in fact take steps to prevent the man, Adam and his wife Eve from getting access to the tree of life. It's interesting that the man, Adam and his wife Eve , have become like the LORD GOD ALMIGHTY in some ways; knowing the difference between good and evil. This was something that the LORD GOD ALMIGHTY had the ability

232

to do. Therefore,in some ways the man, Adam and his wife have in some small way become God - like , which is what the woman, Eve had wanted to do in her eating of the fruit of the forbidden tree.

Verse 23 is interesting, in that, there seems to be a process on show in terms of the removal of the Man and the Woman from the very grounds of the Garden of Eden. The LORD GOD

ALMIGHTY firstly makes the man, Adam work the earth of the Garden of Eden. It is not until verse 24 that the LORD GOD ALMIGHTY fully expels the man,Adam from the confines of the Garden of Eden itself.

Verse 24 is very explicit; ' He drove out the human ' (CEB translation) . The LORD GOD ALMIGHTY drives the Man and the Woman out of the very Garden of Eden that He had placed them in. He definitely did not want them to get access to the very tree of life that was in the Garden of Eden. He takes very strong steps to ensure that this cannot in fact happen. So , in the end the Fall of Mankind as outlined in the narrative of Genesis Three is now complete. There is a breaking of the real and intimate fellowship that the man and the woman and the LORD GOD ALMIGHTY had known in the Garden of Eden.

7.

EPILOGUE :

This book has
the title of; 'Grace :
The Fall From :
Genesis Three'. It
has sought to think

through what Genesis Three : 1 - 24 is all about and what it can and does say to us today in our times and in our generations. The main thing we saw was that the first man and woman made the choice to

disobey the LORD
GOD ALMIGHTY
and His express
words and
commands to them;
by their eating of the
fruit of the tree they
were forbidden to
eat from. The text
itself is very clear in

what it says , as to who is responsible for the actions of the first man and the first woman. The intrusion and work of the talking snake into the pristine and perfect Garden of Eden is

247

and was noted in this book. Yet, even given the intrusion of evil into the Garden of Eden; it was recognized that the first man and the first woman still made their own choices not to obey

the very words and
the commands of the
LORD GOD
ALMIGHTY.

It was also
noted that the woman
had the motivation of
seeking to be like the
LORD GOD. Some
do not make much of

this and yet it would seem to be at the very heart of the moral failure of both the man and the woman in the very Garden of Eden. It's not just that they failed to obey the LORD GOD but also that they wanted to usurp His place in their own lives. They sought to be the LORD GOD ALMIGHTY of their own lives; to break away from His very own control and guidance of their lives.

Also, we have seen the verdicts and the various punishments that the LORD GOD ALMIGHTY gave to the snake, the woman and the man Adam. It was noted that there may well be some thing in the very order of the punishments meted out by the LORD GOD ALMIGHTY. Yet, one does not want to take this too far?

   In the very midst

of the punishments
being meted out
there is in reality the
continued mercy,
love and grace of the
LORD GOD
ALMIGHTY being
shown to the first
man, Adam and the
first woman, Eve.

254

The consequences of the actions of the man and the woman could very well have been much worse and yet the LORD GOD ALMIGHTY in the very midst of judging them shows

255

them much love,
mercy and grace.
The reality, is that,
the LORD GOD
ALMIGHTY does
not in fact have to
do this but He
chooses to show
them these three
things; grace, mercy

and love. He also shows mercy, love and grace to the succeeding generations through them as well.

THE AUTHOR :

JOHN C BURT.

JOHN WORSHIPS AT ST. PHILLIPS, ANGLICAN CHURCH, AUBURN,NSW, AUSTRALIA. HE HAS BEEN THERE A NUMBER OF YEARS ....

267

IT IS A RELATIVELY
LARGE CHURCH
WITH A DIVERSE
MULTI - CULTURAL
CONGREGATION.
ALL OF WHICH
MAKES FOR
GREAT CHURCH
LUNCHES ....

268

JOHN LOVES THE COFFEE IN AUBURN; FROM THE MANY CAFES AND RESTAURANTS THAT ARE THERE. HE LIKES HIS COFFEE TO BE HOT AND STRONG.

269

JOHN ALSO HAS
A FONDNESS
FOR CHICKEN
AND JELLYFISH;
A CHINESE DISH,
WHICH IS VERY
NICE , SERVED
COLD .. AS WELL
AS LOVING THE

270

ODD PIZZA; WITH ANY FORM OF TOPPING THAT IS AVAILABLE AT THE TIME. AS WELL AS LOVING INDIAN FOOD AS WELL .....

271

AMEN AND

AMEN .....

272

SHALOM ...

MAY THE VERY REAL PEACE OF THE LORD JESUS CHRIST RULE YOUR HEARTS AND MINDS ...

AMEN .....

273

280

CPSIA information can be obtained
at www.ICGtesting.com
Printed in the USA
BVHW022016280719

554531BV00011B/463/P

9 780368 105869